The

BEST

Business Advice

YOU

Ever Received

A Quick and Practical Guide to Move You
From Startup to Success!

Preface

The beginning of this book, came into existence from a question I posed on a Social Networking site Alignable back in November 2017. These responses to the question *"What is the BEST Business advice you ever received? Why was it so valuable?"* were put forth from many individuals throughout North America sharing their wisdom.

I imagine much of this wisdom is very old, passed down through the ages. Some may be more valuable than others. Some will resonate with you. Some may irritate or annoy. Some you may not agree with. Some you may look to employ immediately into your business and life design.

Take this wisdom if you can, and leave that which you cannot. As Bruce Lee stated in his Masterpiece *Tao of Jeet Kune Do*

Action is a high road to self-confidence and esteem. Where it is open, all energies flow toward it. It comes readily to most people and its rewards are tangible.

Or to quote the popular NIKE advertisement

Just Do It

Be Well and Enjoy, Namaste – Wes Paterson

The best advice. To follow my dreams and never give up. Ask a lot of questions. Learn from the Experts. Start small and expand. Treat every customer as the only customer. Learn from your mistakes. Offer a solid product, idea, service etc. Your word is your best asset. If your word is not trusted then you are out of luck! Because we all become great after trials and errors!
– Angela Scanion

Always be honest be professional and show appreciation, if you follow this you will always be the best at what you do.
– Russell Vaughan

Yes!
– Paul Ng

Never give up, keep your chin up and keep going forward. My dream is my dream and only I can fulfill it, put God first and all else will follow.
– Kim Warren

Be proactive. Anticipate multiple outcomes. Don't vacillate – say what you mean, and mean what you say. I've found these things very beneficial, and as in life, make for good primary core business values.
– Mark Hitt

Maintain your integrity; build relationships, and deliver on your commitments.
– Bill Daniel

Discover your niche in the business, and do not try to be all things to all people. Be selective in the projects presented, and hone your talent to those particular genres. For me, my money voice is in long form narrations. Secondly, do not under value your own worth. In my business, there are a number of resources available that under value and under cut their services, mainly because they do not have the training and experience to provide true quality work. A highly trained, professional voice, who has invested time, effort and money into having a professional quality studio, will always give you the best value for your money.
– Wayne Edwards

To have balance in my career. Spend more time with God and family first, prioritize my Life. Understand the real qualities of life and the Lord will make sure business and success are in abundance.
– Eric Taylor

Follow the "Golden Rule"... self explanatory
– Gary Celeste

If you don't first believe in your strengths and abilities... then no one else will. Be confident, you are a rock star!
– Bobbi Maxwell

Learn to say the word "No" when I'm not able to do it
– Eva Jones

Communicate: Appreciate: Deliver
The client is a Senior Partner and it is your job to make sure the relationship remains the primary focus and is the essential component for success.
– Sidney Oyola

Be yourself and treat the other the way you want to be treated.
– Rami Hanna

The best advice was and still is important, to be. If you want to earn money from your business the first thing you need to learn is to get and keep customers.
– Ric Ireland

Focus on the RESULTS YOU WANT to achieve, not on the TASKS you think you need to do during the course of the day. Measure the end results you accomplish, not the tasks you check off your to do list.
– Duane Hardy

If you build it, they will come!
– Rabab Al-Amin

There are no rules. Vision is a precursor to reality. Find a way to get it.
– Thad Beverdorf

I saw it on a sign in the successful food retailer Stew Leonard's. The sign said... "Stew Leonard's follows two simple rules. 1. The customer is always right. 2. When in doubt refer to rule #1.
– Neil Brownlee

Never give up and become everyone's friend over the phone or in person, earn their trust!
– Dave Cross

"There are no problems, only opportunities."
I've always loved that quote that a business associate said to me once, and every time I'm in a difficult situation, I try to remember it!
– Janice D. Burness

Listen
– Adam Waldman

First one... "There is no END to Yoga" and I can remember my reaction to my teacher's words. Wait, I thought to myself, isn't the goal of Yoga... Enlightenment!..?..& perfect health. Life happens, learn to flow and consider the power of SLOW... these words, remind me of the value of PERSISTENCE. And one other statement from a friend who worked for the Polaroid Corporation in the last century. It was a game-changer for me, because I was not truly LISTENING. "There is NO FAILURE, only FEEDBACK."
– Sue Anne Willis

Learn from adversity. Every negative comment can have a positive impact especially from experts in your field.
–Frances Stewart

It's been my experience that if you focus on taking care of your customers, your staff, and your suppliers first, they will in turn take care of you.
– Tom Paterson

Remember there is a value to doing business with you, and they will get what they pay for. It's analogous to buying your meal at McDonald's vs. a local restaurant or eatery. Convenience and low cost vs. local friendly service and knowing the person you're dealing with and where the food comes from.
– Walt Reynolds

The best business advice I ever received is, never to spend money on state of the art marketing, but referrals. It says that while state of the art marketing could get your company name all over, it does not really prompt people. But, referrals will surely prompt people to act because it is rewarding to those referring clients to you. While the former might not be totally unproductive the ratio to the latter might be like 1:60%. It is usually an exceptional case that you will receive a contact just because they saw your sign, post or flyer. There is a 60% chance that you will get a referral if anyone on your program sees someone that needs your service.
– Akognon Ojo

Write out your vision… keep looking at it and update.
– Karen Kaye

From my mom: Nothing happens without a decision. Don't be afraid to make them!
– Carole Stein

My law firm has been built on three pillars: (i) Delivery of the utmost cerebral skills, (ii) Total integrity, and (iii) Service throughout. The firm has continued successfully for over 25 years.
– Kenneth Miles

Remember your clients/customers are Most Important, Listen to Them!!
– Troy Bell

Keep at it!
– Alison S. Moran

I guess the best advice I have ever gotten was from my Dad prior to his death. What he said to me although he wasn't a wealthy man, he said I have given you your last name and have taught you that as a young man your word is your bond. If you say you're going to do something, you always follow through with it and do it. I have carried my Dads so called philosophy of life through 26 years of military service as an US Army Aviation Air & Ground Flight Safety Officer, and have continued it throughout the last 20 years as a civilian and sole proprietor of an OSHA Compliance Consulting Company.
– Richard Paul

Learn early the difference between hearing and listening. A person who listens is way more successful than someone who only hears. There is an art to listening. Listening breeds learning. Listening allows for retention. Listening cements prosperity.
– Scott Kahn

Ask?? To customers and their changing needs. Tailor your product to those needs. Give a few free samples to long time customers, See the reactions... Get a terrific media consultant such as Leah Star McMahon.
– Evan Sigmund

Be real! Answer your phone... most of the time... that is the simplest thing you will need to do to win your clients over. Making time for them will show you're committed to their success as well.
– Wade Henderson

To be honest in your sales approach as well as very knowledgeable in your products. Honesty helped me a lot through selling properties, investments, financial services... till now with mortgages. It will retain sales, increase the references and keep your client always satisfied.
– Rola Hamdan

Best business advice: from my dear departed dad. Know your business and be honest with the customer.
– Adrian Humphreys

Best advice, be here a year from now. Consistent and persistent activity leads to long-term results!
- Allison Stillman

Don't be afraid to make a change (personnel, strategies, etc.); don't overwork yourself, make sure you find time for yourself; don't get frustrated when things are not going the direction you want them to go in.
– Joseph Singleton

Best thing I learnt was to get to the shop early and be gone by 1PM, or you are just wasting your time in the office. I was told this by several, big company owners.
– Jeff Mcauliff

Be persistent – in many cases, the more you go after what you want, you will eventually get it and learn along the way.
– Dana Bloom

Believe in yourself!
– Juanita Fewer

The harder you work, the luckier you are.
– John DeBellis

I have been fortunate to have a couple of mentors in my life who just happened to be excellent businessmen.
My father was very successful in virtually everything he touched and provided me with sage advice at an early age.
Don't be too serious in your business dealings and your clients will appreciate doing business with you.
Treat them as you would want to be treated if you were in their shoes.
My second mentor told me not to be a "nice" guy but a "good" guy.
As the saying goes, "nice" guys finish last.
"Nice" guys do everything they can to please their clientele and seldom get rewarded with more business.
"Good" guys will also please their clientele but expect to be rewarded with additional business and ask for it, which, traditionally they do receive.
I am proud to say that, although it was initially difficult for me to do, I now consider myself a "good" guy.
– Samuel Schwartz "Schwartzie"

The best advice I have ever received was "know your worth". A lot of people sell themselves short when it comes to pricing. The second best piece of advice was to always continue education related to your field. It is very important to be an expert in your field so you can provide your customers valuable insight.
– Pamela Baker

Talk to and read about the people that inspire your business model or mission.
– Cynthia Castle

Surround yourself by people who are a lot smarter than you are.
– Scott Fass

Identify your target market-segment, and make sure it can be readily reached via a target message and a product-delivery channel. This saves you from trying to sell high quality TV antennas to folks who don't watch TV.
– Maurice Gull

Be honest and treat people with respect. No bullshit. Every client is important.
– Paul Mann

Honesty
– George Thomas

You're only as good as your last Detail. There are too many who become complacent and inconsistent as time goes on. My work ethic is unyielding. I outperform, and outlast the competition. I deliver every time!
– Andrew O'Keeffe

Know the framework upon which your business is built and stay true to that framework no matter what happens.
– Jay Newman

Always do a great job at a fair price and your customers will help by spreading the word.
– Ernest Girard

Treat every customer the way you want to be treated! I very seldom have a bad situation with a customer!
– Rachel Engel

Plan to work, work your plan, and then your plan will work to success. If the plan does not work, do not change it, go back to the planning table and figure out why, and make the change there. Hip changes are usually disasters.
– Dewey Painter SR

Don't be afraid to ask for referrals.
– Leo Ratmansky

Always ask for referrals.
– Debbie Smith

Provide good customer service and they'll keep coming back. If a customer is not happy with the way you've done something, try to figure out how to fix it. If you can't do that, refund their money immediately with no further questions asked. If your clientele is willing to pay you a fair price for what you provide, don't panhandle them for further reward. Allow them to do this at their discretion. If they tip you 50 dollars, smile and say, "Thank you." If they tip you 5 cents, smile and say, "Thank you." Don't whine. If you do a good job, you'll attract good customers and the bad ones will become few and far between.
– Nicole Chaplain-Pearman

Love what you do.
– Callie P. Roberts

The best business advice that I have received is that failure is an opportunity for success! This really empowered me and my business journey, to the extent that I posted a video and wrote a book chapter on analyzing and turning what was once perceived as a failure into a forward success! I call it #NoFailuresMindshift! Always remember that without a "failure" you won't know what to do to accelerate your success!
– Gwendolyn Davis-Yancey

There are some words which need to be removed from your vocabulary: NO, FAILURE, MISTAKE. Erase them from your head. They will only gain traction if you let them. Their replacements are: YES, POSSIBILITY, RESILIENCE. Follow your instincts and make changes as required. Learn, Learn, Learn.
– Sepp Seitz

The best advice I've received is… do what you love and hire someone else to do the things you don't.
– Lisa Michele Carpenter

Never measure success with money.
– John Gallant

Be honest and fair with pricing a job, give prompt service and don't make a commitment you can't keep.
– Don Gillingham

Golden Rule Always, always, always. Treat others the way you would like to be treated.
– Grant Hawkins

The best business advice that I have ever received was to "eat my own dog food." Basically, if you don't believe in your own product and use your own product – why would anyone else? This also lets you in on how your product could be better.
– Erik Miller

Be the first one to leave.
– Andrea Houtkin

The best advice I received was to always have a paper trail, i.e., put everything in writing. Of course, today that includes electronic communications.
– Stacey Mathis

Knowledge has no power until it's applied.
– Kevin Coombs

Aggressively listen.
– Richard Burtis

You get what you believe you deserve!
– Jay Duquette

A lot of my job is talking with people. When I was first starting out I felt like I could never say anything right. At that point the best business advice I ever received was this:
"You can't say the wrong thing to the right person. Likewise, you can't ever say the right thing to the wrong person!"
Be yourself, love others. You want the RIGHT people on your team. You will reap what you sow.
– Leslee Branson

Keep your promise.
– Trevor Standard

Your word means everything. Keep your promises and conduct yourself with the utmost integrity and ethics. It's most valuable because, every little thing you skip on or do subpar effects all things in your life, personal and business.
– Dale Bunn

Make sure you have a well-designed and informative web site with all contact information.
– Robert Schaefer

Treat others as you want to be treated and hustle every day....
– Joseph Bonaduce

Keep it simple, everything needs to be run by you, keeps it simple.
– Tom Churchill

To stay true to myself and never do anything in business that is unethical, illegal, or immoral. A mentor many years ago showed me that one can be successful by doing the right thing and treating others with respect and dignity.
– Richard Davis

Create a clear mission (purpose), have a vision of the ideal future, keep your focus on the most important outcomes, take care of your health and well-being, never forget that relationships are the magic ingredient, always operate from a position of high integrity, always have a short term and a longer term plan in place, and modify these as needed, don't procrastinate, and follow through on all agreements.
– John Adams

Working with 0.
– George Mikhael

Translators and interpreters are like snipers. We aim for the most accurate term and we never miss.
– Tatiana Raineri

Consistently and carefully plan key objectives that will make a major difference in your business. The daily grind will take over and we will stay stuck in the mud, so each day write on your calendar one objective that will make a difference that day. This advice was and is valuable because it helps me keep my eyes on the goal and not get caught up in the daily stuff.
– Heather Slinkard

Problems are not like wine, they don't get better with age. Communicate and address any issues with your clients or your staff quickly and honestly. Don't put it off – it won't get better on its own!
– Mike Kesler

Cherish the positive and not so positive feedback because they are both a gift. We love all feedback and cherish our customers!
– Ken Tobler

Be honest, keep your word, and remember that your customer is the reason you are in business.
– Scott Roe

Love what you do, and do it like you love. Never work for the money, work for your passion, and the money will come.
– Bryan Evans

As a designer in the Women's fashion industry the best advise I received was about Fabric weights... as there are 240 different temperatures each day in the USA, there is the Mideast the Midwest the South East the South West... as a designer I then started to work with different textiles for each region... and designed the same styles but used different weights of fabric collections for 4 parts of the USA!
– Barbara Hirsh

You can start small, without a large investment and build gradually, like with my business:
http://www.naturalpathremedies.com
- Lorene Benoit

Build your Trust in Business and follow it through in all your dealings.
– Bashir Khan

Read Michael Gerber's E-Myth Revisited.
– Jo Ann Switzer

Relationships are the lifeblood of your business... take care to hone your relationships, both personally and professionally, and you will be grounded and effective.
– Mary E. Madigan

To treat all of your patients as you would like your parents treated by another doctor AND to read the book "The E-Myth".
– Mark Alano, D.C.

The best advice I ever received was from an old mentor of mine. He said regarding selling, "there's a long way from the mouth to the pocketbook".
– Michael Riso

To buy my own button machine. DIY is how we operate.
– David Gerbstadt

"Call them like you see them! Develop your intuition & listen to your gut. Sometimes that inner voice is your best mentor." Good intuition results in decisive action and past mistakes only help build better intuition and a greater sense of direction. ....So – work on calling them like you see them!
– Adam Rooke

Be honest & informed by valid & reliable sources. Don't sell yourself short. Be a good listener & cater to each client as an individual with individual issues, needs, and goals. Admit when you don't have a true answer, and promise to get back to that client with the answer, ASAP. Treat others' as you would want to be treated, with respect. Take the time needed to gather critical information about your client. Do what you love, motivated by passion & not by money.
– Betty Craven

The best advice I ever received came from a great Mentor – no matter how much I knew, I knew who to listen to and I took what I learned and never forgot the advice – Bottom line, find or when you find a mentor listen, learn, adapt and then make it your own.
☺
- Larry Kudeviz

The very best advice I've ever received came to me within the past few weeks. The advice, to look inside myself, understand how truly amazing of a person I am, realize how much I have to give to many people and to realize this and move forward with this new knowing of myself, step outside my own box and make things happen, help people that are still sick, suffering and dying at an alarming rate.
– Bob Wade

Remember – advice you receive is directly influenced by the adviser's compensation plan. If you are seeking trustworthy advice, find a neutral source to get it.
– Rick Fearman

Always treat the client with the utmost respect; learn from every experience and always be honest and above board. Most of all... believe in yourself.
– Sharon Siegel

Start getting ready for the New Year at least (2) months early. Start with a CPOT audit of your books and payroll. If you have an LLC, make sure it is owned by a C-Corp for the best protection. If your business is sole-owned, there is an 85% chance you will be audited. By being a C-Corp, you will lower your chance of an audit by 85%.
– William Goff

Always be honest. No matter the circumstances, everyone can work together to resolve problems, if they know of the issues at hand.
– Ashley DeHaven

Be kind... treat customers like you want to be treated. Be fair with pricing and you will always get repeat customers. Most of our business comes from word of mouth advertising.
– Janice Anderson

Make friends, not enemies!
– Donald Hoblitzell

See this link for your plan
http://www.entrepreneur.com/article/247540
- Kathleen McDowell

Best advice... Be passionate about what you do! Passion removes the four-letter word we may drop from time to time – WORK! It's not work, if you love it!!!!
– V. Tina Carini

As business owners we still are 'employed' by consumers to keep growing. Always encourage positive customer service as they can 'make or break' your biz via social media feedback.
– Melanye Maclin MD

Be sure you are well funded for 6 months and willing to work long hours.
– Doyle Fain

Adopt to new trends and respond to market changes as quickly as it happens. Make your processes more efficient and effective to avoid waste to become more profitable. You need to review your processes over the time as you grow your business to replace all that are not working well for you and your customers. I made these changes over the past two years and seen a significant growth on my bottom line.
– Ali Moshajari

Be true to yourself and realistic in your goals.
– Linda Odom

Always put yourself in the buyer's shoes. Stop thinking about your commission or profit and think about how you can help this person realize their goal.
– Harry Peterson

I was told by a successful business woman who is mentoring me that, "You have everything within you that you need to succeed!" It was a game changer for me!
– Cathleen Baker

Know what your customer wants and make it personal.
– Rita Monette

"Figures don't lie.... Only liars figure!"
Follow the numbers, make peace with your bottom line.
– Ali R. Rodriguez

Don't over leverage a commercial property purchase. If you do, you could lose the property in a sharp downturn like 2009. 65% LTV is a good guideline.
– Mark Birmingham

1. *Never give up. Never ever, ever, ever, give up.*
2. *Know when to quit. If you're digging yourself a hole quit digging.*
3. *KNOW THE DIFFERENCE BETWEEN THE TWO.*
4. *Read "How To Win Friends and Influence People" by Dale Carnegie. It changed my life.*
5. *Never stop learning.*
6. – Bill Myers

Never go into a partnership business, 50/50 doesn't work and they were correct.
– Ralph C. Pennington

Learn all you can and remember it is about helping people and doing what you can to get their lives back on track.
– Tammara Abbott

I learned this one the hard way, in the trenches and then observed this in the marketplace. The size of business that is the hardest to run are medium-sized businesses. Small businesses can be run out of a home, overhead can be low, and it is not as hard to find talented workers when you only have a few. Large businesses have sales volume to cover overhead, employee perks, and they have figured out how to build a competitive advantage. When a firm takes a step up in overhead, they are squeezed on both ends.

I was in a construction business. The first business started with 4 employees and then we jumped to 15. Everything became more challenging as we grew including overhead costs for an office, driving distances to customer sites, invoice payment timing from customers, and labor supply. We closed the business, reorganized, and came up with a way to have true competitive advantage. Everything changed. Everyone wanted our business, we grew rapidly to one of the largest firms in the country for our type of business, customers paid their bills rapid fast, were able to hire the best people, we had volume efficiencies, we were able to negotiate material input discounts. Work was fun.

– Susan Thrower

Underestimate and over deliver! Always give a little extra to the job!

– Jana Schreiber

Planning is the key to success. Knowing how you can fit the pieces of your business together (marketing, finance, HR, technology and product/service) into a coherent sustainable plan will guarantee success.
– Edward Siegel

Secure URLs containing the best key words for your business in terms of search engine optimization. Point these URLs to your business website. Worth its weight in gold and then some. You should have to spend very little in advertising after you do this.
– Greg Dueck

To know your products and why they help people so much… I was a writer, worked for companies in Chicago, NYC, but had never had me own business & not one where products were involved, so that helped.
– Diane Pellettiere

Tailor providing a service to the varying needs of the client. Client is more likely to stay with you even when having difficulties.
– Bruce Trudel

Give your client your full attention.
– Joel Pasternack

Knowing where the market is going is one thing.
Capitalizing on that knowledge is another.
As consumers continue to transition their buying power to the
online marketplace, companies that have the greatest strategic
position are poised to capture the largest share.
– Eric Aldrin

Provide real time solutions to your clients immediate needs, then
help them incorporate long term strategies to grow their
business and create leverage to build on.
– James Guerra

It doesn't matter what medium you use (they are merely tools), it
is how you present your message. It must touch an emotional
cord with your audience.
– Clive Branson

Everyone is not your customer, you win some you lose some; stay
focused and move to the next one; every customer deserves 100%
of your efforts. It has helped me gain and retain more customers.
– Ken

There is always a solution, it's often just silencing the noise to
hear it.
– Karla Ferster

Keep ahead of the trends, or at least keep up with them.
– Paul Orozco

Include God in all your decisions.
Just when I think I am doing the right thing or know the right
answer is when I am reminded that without Him, I am nothing.
– Kevin Cate

Dick Merrill once told me that you are never "going" to do
anything. You are either doing it or you have done it. Saying that
you are going to do something means that you are not taking it
seriously enough.
– Bill Barlow

"Half of the battle is just showing up." Not showing up to work at
all can be tempting when you own your own business. The
problem is, if you don't show up to work, your business suffers –
and you don't eat. Getting yourself out of the house and to the
office in the morning will kickstart your day. You're bound to be
more productive because you're not distracted with TV, your
comfy couch, or the unwashed dishes in the kitchen (I
procrastinate by cleaning my house). As an entrepreneur, this
was valuable because it taught me that I have the ultimate say in
the success of my company. The words are not only simple, but
they're incredibly empowering; I hope you find it that way, too.
– Jave Bjorkman

Never Assume anything. It is too easy to find out information.
– Nelson Gill

Never hire a family member and never ever use designated business capital for personal use. Stay focused on things to do, personal goals and business plan. "Eat beans – no steak."
– Bruce Terrell

You are judged by the company you keep...
- Rick Carlson

Be committed to your business goals and do the A's each day.
– David Zimmerman

Best business advise ever was to NEVER treat the customer wrong and go the extra mile to keep them happy!
– Ron Zant

Always lead with pain, followed by the relief: "We work with clients who are particularly challenged with growing their business. They have tried various tactics but still do not see top line growing. Our services seek to understand the obstacles to growth, align your company's strategy with markets of choice and drive revenue growth 20%+ year over year." People care less about what you do, and care most about what they GET when they engage you. Talk about "outcomes."
– Tim Steele

Every business has a life stage, and your tasks and strategies will have to align with the life stage of the business.
– Bonnie Lee

Don't listen to others, do what YOU think is right. Never doubt yourself and never give up.
– Conny Manero

Best advice? Stop looking for advice from others until I understand that ALL success begins within. BEST ADVICE I ever got.
– David Breslow

Take care of your employees and they will take care of your customers.
– Cindy Bearden

Have clarity about what you want (your most important goals) and priorities should follow in moving you in the direction of your most important goals.
– Jim Flemming

The best business advice I ever received was/is "If your WHY doesn't make you cry, it's not big enough." That is to say that if the ultimate reason that you are in business (after "achieving fame and fortune") does not speak to your very heart, then it is not accurately your big WHY. Your why has to be important enough to get you out of bed every day, even when you don't feel like it. Your why is what keeps you going, when you are done and done. Your why should make you cry when you think about it and definitely when you talk about it. What is your why and does it make you cry?
– Charlie Lee

Love what you do!
– Kevin House

Be honest... It's difficult to remember a lie.
– W.J. (Bill) Chafee

Be honest in all that you do. Customers value genuine people. If you can develop an attitude of honesty, hard work, and a desire to make customers feel that they are important to you... then the sky is the limit in having customer loyalty and satisfaction. Success will be in your sights continually.
– Bill Fairbanks

Always treat your customers like they are Number 1 and don't be afraid to ask for referral from them.
– Maryose Cokeley

The more failure you have, the more growth you will experience!
– John Riley III

In business, head before heart... but don't ever lose your heart.
– Dr. Bob Gordon

Hire good people and get out of their way.
– Liam Maddock

People buy from people.
– Diana Dejacimo

Always Be Prospecting!
– Anthony Agbro

My best advice was don't fear failure or making a mistake. That is the true positive feedback to move on.
– Hasson Diggs

1 - Find joy in a portion of what you do. 2 - Tenacity – never give up, ever.
– Paul Page

NO means – New Opportunity
– Joel Ehrlich

"No" is one step closer to a "Yes"
– Tracy Gibson

Yes in regards to Food Safety and Quality.
– Goranka Platisa

Treat others as you would want to be treated. Best advice ever.
– Judy Walters

There is no limit to the amount of good one can do if they don't care who gets the credit.
The mentor who taught this to me was a master seed planter. He would plant seeds in people's minds of action or strategy to take, nurture the ideas, until they blossomed in the minds of the people as their own ideas.
I watched him literally change the world with this process in a massive, global NGO. While, I never became as adept as he was, I have used this to change people and organizations for 2 decades.
– Larry Stevenson MPA

Indecision hurts you more than a wrong decision. The mark of a true professional isn't whether you make mistakes but your reaction and how you correct those mistakes.
– Dana Horne

The book "Think and grow Rich" – "It take White Hot Heat" to finish the race.
– Bud Jones

How I can work from home and built my personal business.
– Patricia Elizabeth Miranda

JUST DO IT!!
- LeRoy St. Germaine

Mine, was to "Incorporate myself as a business"... good from a tax standpoint.
– Jim Caron

The best advice I received is to believe in yourself, dream and business venture. Appreciate all customers, referrals and be open to suggestions about increasing revenue and business. Do not over extend yourself! It's okay to turn down customers and contracts if you don't have the bandwidth to cover them all. Trust and build solid relationships.
– Darius Hall

Mind your own.
– Ben Gill

Keep your overhead low, always communicate promptly, the customer is always right, take the utmost pride in your work, make those around you feel special, treat everyone as you wish to be treated and then still take it to a notch higher.
– Dan Hegarty

Document interactions with higher ups and co-workers, because people are not truthful. And silence can never be misquoted...
- Marcia McDonald

The advice was to go ahead and do it. Don't wait for approval. As an author that is a new concept.
– Steve Shapiro

Be honest, ethical, respectful, fair... Why? It's the only way to truly do business.
– Anthony Ferrigno

My best business advice is to focus on the one thing you enjoy the most, are an expert in, are willing to put long hours doing it, and then go for it.
– Lorna Hunter

If you can't walk into a room of 100 strangers and come away with 50-60 business cards you shouldn't be in business for yourself.
– Ken Galo

Just be yourself and always leave your clients with a smile on their face.
– Craig Zaffe

Always treat people with respect independently of their citizenship, race, social status, gender or beliefs... After more than 20 years of expatriation around the world I believe this was the most valuable advice...
- Phillippe Richez

An old man told me what his dad said for business advice: "If you get out of bed every morning and go to work, you're bound to make some money" It speaks to hunger to succeed. It all starts with hunger.
– Norman Bacheldor

Show client your credentials! Be Honest and up front. Listen more than speaking. If you don't know the answer (being upfront) then research it and get back to them. Be a better listener than speaker!
– Daniel Heskett

It's not what you know, but what you do with what you know. It was so valuable because you don't have to be a rocket scientist but you do need to take action and be diligent in order to be successful.
– Joan Wiederspiel

As I was leaving home to enter the US Navy, my dear Mom said... Lenny, wherever you go, whomever you meet, and whatever you do... MAKE NICE! It's worked well so far.
– Len Kaine

The most valuable business advice I ever received is that no person can build a business alone, but they can build a winning team to succeed. As part of that I was told to make each role clear and concise as to what the expectation were and what freedom they had to meet their individual challenge.
– Harold Mindlin

Worry about yourself and don't worry about the other guy.
– Fred Boucher

Do what you do best, and hire the rest.
– Juli Schatz

The first advice I received from my father: never be late for an appointment. Come 10 min before, go to the washroom, check your appearance and at the right time (by minutes) be at the reception desk. Be dressed accordingly – never overdressed or the opposite. I have been in business about 63 years. Never was late for an appointment. You must be organized and know exactly what you need or what you would like to achieve. This is the first step of your success.
– Anna Mordukhovich

Make a decision! Don't hesitate, if the decision is wrong you will probably have enough time to recover. If it is the right decision you are that much further ahead.
– Mike Ferrari

Always pay yourself and always be willing to teach/give back free information... remember someone gave it to you and there's enough to go around!
– Jaynette Lancaster

Contact the previous satisfied customers, they are the best references you can have.
– Nicole Renwick

Hire people who are smarter than you, and always be educated from them.
– Dmitriy Teryokhin

Trust in yourself. If you are relying on support from others because you do not feel you are credible... work for someone else.
– Arthur Taft

Listen to your "customer", playback what you heard verbally to show you are listening and for alignment and then follow-up throughout the process to ensure results are attained. Remember names of people you meet and address them with their name. Build trust and integrity... do what you say you're going to do and do it well. Plus, my grandfather's advice was lead, follow, or get the hell out of the way.
– Dennis McKinney

Believe and trust in yourself.
– Robert (Bob) Dahl

Find a business that you can perform with passion. The ethical business always has a win / win outcome.
– Antonia Lineaweaver

The best advice I ever got was: "Do what you are passionate about and success will follow. Don't focus on money, but on what you love to do!"
– Christine O'Keefe

Always think about what is best for the other person and never give them less, even if someone else has what is best for them. Tell them who that is and get them together.
- Wesley Zimmerman

*I never received advice from anyone. I started everything myself.
My best advice, be honest, be 100% transparent, be absolutely
yourself and always wear a warm smile. This all builds
foundation of trust, that builds a bridge to true lasting
friendships. "Success without integrity means nothing!"*
– Daniel Gard

*Remember it is NOT about you. Be a consultative sales person
and ask your prospective client what their specific needs are in
making an investment. Also, find out more about their
background and make sure you match their background
experience with your prospective client's professional
experiences and business request needs. Then tailor a match that
will meet their criteria.*
– Dick Humphrey

*The best advice I received was to keep my clients' interests first
and foremost, and be responsive to their questions, needs and
concerns. I have endeavored to do this in my law practice and it
has helped me stay in business for over twenty years.*
– Les Romo

*Always be like a sponge. Always remain coachable and keep
pushing.*
– Robert Jordan

That's a great question. Lots of answers could be put here. But the best business advice I've ever received is in God's Word. Philippians 2:14 says, "Do all things without grumbling or complaining."
Of course this isn't just what you say, it's what's in your heart. Sounds too simple, but when you depend upon Jesus For His thankfulness, and just simply ask Him to help you with it, He will. It's impossible to be perfect in anything. So when I fail at being thankful, and want to complain, I ask Jesus to forgive me, and He does. He is my ever present help in every time of need. That's the best advice I've been given. Hope you have a great day. In Christ,
- Jason Snobeck

Don't ever forget what made you success.
– Linda Ivanoff

When you are passionate about your service/product, that passion shows and people are naturally drawn to hear your message. You can't rest on your past achievements, as you are only as valuable as what you offer your customer today and each day.
– Katie Gilfeather

To get an address book and put in it everyone I meet who might be able to be of assistance in the future and what they can offer.
– Ed Weems

I am a designer/salesperson/manager. The best advise that I have ever been given for business is that I should sell myself, not my product because in essence the prospective client is buying <u>you, not the product</u>. They can get that product from anywhere, but they can't get you anywhere! Be as genuine, honest, straightforward, personable and professional as you can possibly be without being a fake or a "salesman". People can detect a fake a mile away! Form a professional relationship and connection with the prospective client and make them want to buy from you because that is what it's really about!
– Dennis R. Costa

Solve Problems for other people. Always!
- Rebecca Gebhardt Brizi

Plan. Always make plans. Circumstances will change things, and the plans will need to change to take advantage of those changes, but if you don't plan you tend to miss opportunities, lack the structure to make things successful in the long-run, and you ensure that you're constantly running to catch up rather than moving toward your goals.
– Dave Kaplan

By low, sell high.
– Kelly Laurence

No matter who you are doing business with, even family or friends (or should I say, especially?), ALWAYS have paperwork (agreements, contracts). Having the proper business paperwork in place saves you from the inevitable "fails" and allows you the opportunity to learn from your mistakes without having to start from zero. It was so important because it's saved me several times, and more importantly, it's saved my business relationships.
- Rick Shute

Best advice is to give the best customer service possible with integrity and honesty.
– Craig Beckman

Someone once told me that "you can only do what you can do". I found that advice extremely beneficial because as a hard worker I always felt that I pushed myself beyond my limits and capabilities. That one sentence has stuck with me for so many years because now I still do my best job, however I do not have to be completely stressed doing it.
– Lisa Vannata

Go into practice where you are needed and live in the community where you work.
– Dr. Robert Lombardo

The best advice I ever heard? Don't listen to advice...! Not mine, I stole that one. But I liked it!
– Steve Palmer

Don't do business with family or friends, and everything should be ok.
– Gordon Maheu

Be on time, courteous, and deliver a good product.
- Phil De Anda

Treat each and every customer like it was your own family. Customer Service is the most important part of the sale.
– Paul Sikora

Keep pushing through adversity! If you allow adversity to stop you, you will never achieve the goal that YOU set!
- Bobby Jackson

Look around you, everything you see, touch, even the things you've incorporated into your own life, such as the places you've worked, schools attended, cars purchased, the clothes worn, all started as someone's dream. Now serve as evidence that dreams do come true. If theirs can, so can yours.
– Anthony Cooper

If it's hard to accomplish, you will find the most value in the result.
– Kurt Mason

My best business advice comes from my intuition.
- George Russell

You're only as good as your last Detail. There are too many who become complacent and inconsistent as time goes on. My work ethic is unyielding. I outperform, and outlast the competition. I deliver every time!
– Andrew O'Keeffe

To do the best that you can until you know better then better and never be afraid to fail.
– John Joubert

Let your management fix their own mistakes so they learn and grow. Otherwise they become lazy and gun shy and won't make decisions on their own.
– Marcus Giordano

Be true to yourself, be yourself. If you try to maintain a false image or try to be someone or something you are not, it will show. It's not something you can maintain. So don't try to do things like another company just because they have success – it it's not you, it will never work!
– Laura Polegato

Go into business for yourself! It's all worth the satisfaction of claiming yourself.
– Donald Messing

Be true to yourself, stand your ground, and invest in real estate.
– Richard Pichardo

I learned something very early on that is not as easy as it may seem as a sales person because we are loaded with knowledge, and excitement when we visit prospects. I learned to listen! It is that simple, but usually easier said than done. Customers have lots to say when they are given the opportunity.
– Jim DeMichele

Do what you love, don't worry about the money. Because doing what you hate for a "paycheck" just sucks your soul, doing what you love helps you feel passion about work, and make it not seem so much like work. The money will follow.
– Rich Morris

Summary & Conclusion

Advice is great, and as you know, its true value happens when it is taken and applied to YOUR life. As you read this book I am sure certain 'themes' and 'concepts' would have came up for you. There is a reason for that. The advice that repeatedly came up and came forth for YOU came on purpose. NOW is the time to take ACTION and follow the advice you have learned. This book is designed to be read, and re-read many times. Often we need to hear, see, and feel information at least six times for us to properly retain and utilize it. I encourage you to return to this book often. Take what you can use, leave that which you cannot, it is there for another.

I would also like to extend another personal thanks to all of the contributors that shared their wisdom within these pages. I encourage those of you reading to also share the best advice you ever received on business, life, relationships, marriage, friendships, and anything that you found valuable and inspirational thus far during your time here on planet earth. Share your wisdom at bestbusinessadviceever@gmail.com. I look forward to reading YOUR BEST ADVICE!

Cheers;

Wes

The BEST Business Advice YOU ever received

www.ingramcontent.com/pod-product-compliance
Lightning Source LLC
Chambersburg PA
CBHW021045180526
45163CB00005B/2291